Embracing Authenticity

Building Meaningful Relationships with Trans Women

Evelyn R. Beacham

We include personal anecdotes, case studies, and expert insights to provide diverse perspectives and practical advice. By addressing both the emotional and practical aspects of relationships with trans women, this guide aims to foster understanding, respect, and love that transcends societal barriers.

CONTENTS

We will provide readers with a comprehensive understanding of building healthy, supportive relationships with trans women, emphasizing the importance of overcoming societal barriers

1 MEANINGFUL RELATIONSHIPS

Building meaningful relationships with trans women requires genuine connection, acceptance, and a commitment to understanding their unique experiences. This chapter delves into the importance of authenticity in fostering such relationships, offering insights and practical guidance to cultivate deep, respectful, and supportive connections.

Understanding Authenticity in Relationships

Authenticity involves being true to oneself and others, fostering trust and openness. In relationships with trans women, authenticity means recognizing and honoring their identities without preconceived notions or biases. It's about engaging sincerely, free from societal stereotypes, and embracing each individual's unique journey.

The Role of Acceptance

Acceptance is foundational in any relationship, more so when societal prejudices exist. Trans women often face discrimination and misunderstanding; thus, accepting them wholly—acknowledging their gender identity, experiences, and expressions—is crucial. This acceptance fosters a safe space where they feel valued and respected.

Overcoming Societal Barriers

Societal norms and prejudices can hinder authentic connections. To transcend these barriers:

- **Educate Yourself**: Learn about transgender identities, histories, and challenges. Understanding the context helps in empathizing and supporting trans women effectively.

- **Challenge Personal Biases**: Reflect on and address any internalized prejudices. Personal growth is essential for building genuine relationships.

- **Advocate for Inclusivity**: Support policies and practices that promote equality and challenge discrimination against trans individuals.

Effective Communication

Open and respectful communication is vital. This includes:

- **Using Correct Pronouns and Names**: Always address trans women by their chosen names and pronouns, affirming their identity. Misgendering can be harmful and disrespectful.

<u>Hudson Weekly</u>

- **Active Listening**: Pay close attention to their experiences and feelings without judgment. This fosters understanding and trust.

- **Discussing Boundaries**: Have open conversations about comfort levels and boundaries to ensure mutual respect.

Building Trust and Emotional Intimacy

Trust is the cornerstone of any meaningful relationship. To build trust with trans women:

- **Be Consistent**: Show reliability in your words and actions.

- **Respect Privacy**: Understand that sharing one's trans identity is personal. Avoid disclosing someone's trans status without explicit consent.

- **Offer Support**: Be present during challenges, offering emotional and practical support as needed.

Navigating Intimacy

Intimacy involves understanding and respecting each other's bodies and boundaries. For trans women, this may include:

- **Understanding Dysphoria**: Recognize that body dysphoria can affect comfort levels with physical intimacy. Engage in open dialogues about what feels right.

- **Prioritizing Consent**: Ensure that all intimate activities are consensual, with ongoing communication about comfort and boundaries.

Celebrating Individuality

Each trans woman has a unique story and identity. Celebrate their individuality by:

- **Encouraging Self-Expression**: Support their choices in expressing their gender identity, whether through fashion, pronouns, or other means.

- **Valuing Their Experiences**: Acknowledge and honor the experiences that have shaped who they are.

Conclusion

Embracing authenticity in relationships with trans women involves genuine connection, acceptance, and a commitment to understanding and supporting their identities. By overcoming societal barriers, communicating effectively, and building trust, we can cultivate meaningful and enriching relationships that honor the true selves of all individuals involved.

Sources

2 EVOLUTION OF TRANS WOMEN

Trans women have long navigated a complex landscape of societal barriers and challenges, shaped by historical contexts and compounded by discrimination and prejudice. Understanding this intricate history is crucial to fostering genuine connections and acceptance in relationships with trans women.

Historical Context: Evolution of Trans Women's Representation and Rights

The journey of trans women's representation and rights is marked by both progress and persistent challenges. In the early 20th century, individuals like Roberta Cowell, the first known British trans woman to undergo gender-reassignment surgery in 1951, began to emerge publicly, challenging societal norms. However, such milestones were often met with resistance and limited understanding.

<u>All About Law</u>

The late 20th and early 21st centuries witnessed significant strides, with increased visibility of trans individuals in media and the enactment of legal protections. Despite these advancements, trans women continue to face systemic obstacles, including restrictive legislation and societal exclusion. For instance, recent legal battles, such as the U.K. Supreme Court's deliberation on whether trans women can be legally recognized as female, highlight ongoing debates surrounding trans rights.

<u>Them</u>

Discrimination and Prejudice: The Impact of Transmisogyny and Intersectionality

Trans women often encounter unique forms of discrimination rooted in both transphobia and misogyny, a phenomenon known as transmisogyny. This dual bias manifests in various ways, from questioning the legitimacy of trans women's identities to subjecting them to heightened scrutiny and violence.

Intersectionality further complicates these experiences, as factors such as race, socioeconomic status, and disability intersect with gender identity, leading to compounded discrimination. Trans women of color, for example, face disproportionately high rates of violence and incarceration, reflecting the interplay of racism and transmisogyny.

World Without Genocide

Navigating Societal Barriers in Relationships
Building meaningful relationships with trans women necessitates an awareness of these societal barriers and a commitment to overcoming them. Key considerations include:

- **Education and Awareness**: Engaging with resources that explore trans histories and experiences fosters empathy and understanding. For instance, exploring the rich histories of gender-nonconforming individuals can provide valuable context.

- **Challenging Personal Biases**: Reflecting on and addressing one's own prejudices is essential. This involves recognizing how societal norms may have influenced perceptions of gender and actively working to unlearn discriminatory attitudes.

- **Advocacy and Allyship**: Supporting trans rights through advocacy and standing against discriminatory practices contributes to a more inclusive society, benefiting personal relationships and the broader community.

By acknowledging the historical and societal challenges that trans women face, individuals can cultivate relationships grounded in genuine connection and acceptance, paving the way for more inclusive and supportive interactions.

.

Building respectful and supportive relationships with trans women requires intentional communication, active listening, empathy, and trust. These elements are foundational to fostering genuine connections that honor and affirm the identities and experiences of trans women.

Effective Communication

Using correct pronouns and names is a fundamental aspect of respectful interaction. Addressing someone by their chosen name and pronouns validates their identity and demonstrates respect. Misgendering, whether intentional or accidental, can cause significant distress and undermine trust. To ensure respectful communication:

- **Ask and Use Correct Pronouns:** Politely inquire about a person's pronouns if you're uncertain, and consistently use them. This practice shows respect and supports an inclusive environment.

ADL

- **Introduce Your Own Pronouns:** Sharing your pronouns when introducing yourself can create a space where others feel comfortable sharing theirs, normalizing the practice.

Transactual

- **Avoid Assumptions:** Do not assume someone's gender based on appearance or name. When in doubt, ask respectfully.

National Gender Training

Navigating Conversations About Gender Identity

Engaging in discussions about gender identity requires sensitivity and openness:

- **Educate Yourself:** Take the initiative to learn about transgender identities and issues. This reduces the burden on trans individuals to educate others and shows a commitment to understanding.

Transgender Equality

- **Respect Privacy:** Recognize that aspects of a person's transition or identity may be private. Avoid intrusive questions, and allow them to share what they're comfortable with.

Transgender Equality

- **Listen and Validate:** If a trans woman shares her experiences, listen attentively and acknowledge her feelings. Validation fosters trust and connection.

Psychology Today

Active Listening and Empathy

Active listening involves fully concentrating on what is being said rather than passively hearing the message. This practice, coupled with empathy, is crucial in understanding and supporting trans women:

- **Be Present:** Engage in conversations without distractions, showing genuine interest in the person's experiences.

Care Learning

- **Reflect and Clarify:** Paraphrase what has been shared to ensure understanding and ask clarifying questions when necessary.

Care Learning

- **Show Empathy:** Acknowledge the emotions and challenges expressed, offering support and understanding.

Psychology Today

Establishing Trust

Trust is the cornerstone of any meaningful relationship. To build and maintain trust with trans women:

- **Respect Boundaries:** Understand and honor personal boundaries regarding topics of discussion, physical space, and levels of disclosure.

<u>**Transgender Equality**</u>

- **Ensure Confidentiality**: Keep personal information shared in confidence private, unless given explicit permission to share.

<u>**Transgender Equality**</u>

- **Be Consistent and Reliable:** Demonstrate dependability through consistent actions and words, reinforcing reliability.

<u>**Care Learning**</u>

- **Support Autonomy:** Encourage and respect a trans woman's autonomy in making decisions about her life and identity.

<u>**Transgender Equality**</u>

By integrating these practices into interactions, individuals can cultivate respectful and supportive relationships with trans women, contributing to a more inclusive and understanding society.

Navigating intimacy and sexual relationships with trans women requires a nuanced understanding of consent, comfort, and the unique experiences that may influence these interactions.

By fostering open communication, acknowledging the impact of gender dysphoria, and exploring diverse sexual practices with mutual respect, partners can cultivate fulfilling and affirming connections. Consent and Comfort

Establishing clear communication about comfort levels and consent is fundamental in any intimate relationship, and it holds particular significance when one partner is a trans woman. Traditional sexual scripts often fail to encompass the experiences of transgender individuals, necessitating a more personalized approach to consent.

- **Explicit Communication:** Engaging in open dialogues about desires, boundaries, and consent ensures that both partners feel respected and understood. This practice is crucial in navigating the complexities of intimacy, as it allows for the expression of individual needs and concerns.

- **Continuous Consent:** Recognizing that consent is an ongoing process is vital. Regular check-ins during intimate encounters can help partners remain attuned to each other's comfort levels, fostering a safe and responsive environment.

- **Cultural Sensitivity:** Understanding that expressions of consent can vary across cultures is important. Being mindful of these differences and prioritizing clear communication can bridge potential gaps in understanding.

Understanding Dysphoria

Gender dysphoria, characterized by distress due to a mismatch between one's gender identity and assigned sex at birth, can significantly impact intimate relationships. Awareness and sensitivity to this experience are essential for supportive partnerships.

- **Acknowledge Individual Experiences:** Recognize that gender dysphoria manifests differently for each person. Engaging in conversations about how it affects your partner can lead to more empathetic and tailored support.

- **Create Affirming Environments:** Fostering spaces where your partner feels seen and respected in their gender identity can alleviate dysphoric feelings. This includes using correct pronouns and affirming language consistently.

- **Support Access to Care:** Encouraging and facilitating access to gender-affirming healthcare can be instrumental in reducing dysphoria and enhancing overall well-being.

Exploring Sexual Practices

Sexual intimacy is a deeply personal experience, and exploring it with a trans partner involves understanding and respecting diverse practices and preferences.

- **Educate Yourself:** Taking the initiative to learn about transgender experiences and sexual health can reduce misconceptions and promote a more informed approach to intimacy.

- **Prioritize Mutual Satisfaction:** Engage in open discussions about what brings pleasure to each partner. This collaborative approach ensures that intimacy is fulfilling and consensual for both individuals.

- **Be Adaptable:** Recognize that preferences and comfort levels may evolve over time. Maintaining flexibility and openness to change can strengthen the intimate connection.

By integrating these practices, partners can navigate the complexities of intimacy with trans women, fostering relationships built on trust, respect, and mutual satisfaction.

5 SUPPORT

Supporting a partner through their transition is a profound journey that encompasses both medical and social dimensions. It requires a deep commitment to understanding the complexities involved and actively participating as an ally.

Medical and Social Aspects of Transition

Transitioning is a multifaceted process that varies for each individual. It may include medical interventions, social changes, or both, depending on personal needs and circumstances.

- **Hormone Therapy:** Many trans women opt for hormone replacement therapy (HRT) to develop secondary sexual characteristics aligned with their gender identity. HRT can lead to physical changes such as breast development and skin softening. It's essential to understand that these changes occur gradually and can have emotional and physical side effects.

- **Surgical Interventions:** Some may pursue surgeries like breast augmentation or gender confirmation surgery (GCS). These procedures are significant and require comprehensive medical consultations, psychological evaluations, and substantial recovery periods.

- **Social Transition:** This involves changes such as adopting a new name, using different pronouns, and altering one's appearance to reflect their gender identity. Social transition is a critical aspect of affirming one's identity and can present challenges, including navigating societal reactions and potential discrimination.

Throughout these processes, emotional support is paramount. Being present, patient, and understanding can significantly alleviate the stress associated with transition.

Being an Ally

Active allyship involves more than passive support; it requires proactive engagement and advocacy.

- **Educate Yourself:** Take the initiative to learn about transgender experiences and issues. This self-education demonstrates respect and reduces the emotional labor placed on your partner to explain their identity.

Transgender Equality

- **Use Affirming Language:** Consistently use your partner's chosen name and pronouns. This practice validates their identity and fosters a supportive environment.

Transgender Equality

- **Provide Emotional Support**: Be available to listen and offer comfort. Acknowledge the challenges they face and celebrate their milestones.

Love Is Respect

- **Advocate for Their Rights:** Stand up against discrimination and support policies that promote equality. Your advocacy can extend to correcting misconceptions and educating others.

Transgender Equality

- **Respect Their Autonomy**: Recognize that the transition journey is deeply personal. Support your partner's decisions regarding their transition without imposing your expectations.

Plume

- **Seek Support for Yourself:** Engaging with support groups or counseling can help you process your feelings and better support your partner. Understanding your emotions is crucial to maintaining a healthy relationship.

Verywell Mind

By embracing these practices, you not only support your partner but also contribute to a more inclusive and understanding society. Your role as an ally is instrumental in fostering an environment where trans women can thrive authentically.

6 NAVIGATING CHALLENGES

Navigating external challenges is crucial when fostering respectful and supportive relationships with trans women. This involves effectively managing family and social dynamics and being vigilant about safety considerations.

Family and Social Dynamics

Introducing a trans partner to family and friends can present unique challenges, including potential conflicts or misunderstandings. To navigate these dynamics:

- **Open Communication**: Initiate conversations with family members to share your partner's identity and your commitment to the relationship. Providing clear and accurate information can help dispel misconceptions.

- **Education and Resources**: Offer educational materials to family and friends to enhance their understanding of transgender identities. Encourage them to engage with support groups or counseling services to address their concerns and foster acceptance. Organizations like Depend provide support to families and friends of trans individuals, facilitating understanding and acceptance.

<u>Depend</u>

- **Set Boundaries**: Clearly define acceptable behaviors and language regarding your partner's identity. Address any disrespectful comments or actions promptly to maintain a supportive environment.

- **Seek Professional Guidance**: If conflicts persist, consider involving a counselor experienced in LGBTQ+ issues to mediate discussions and provide strategies for fostering acceptance. Professional guidance can be instrumental in navigating complex family dynamics.

Safety Considerations

Trans women often face heightened risks of discrimination and violence. To ensure safety:

- **Awareness of Risks**: Understand that trans individuals may encounter harassment or violence in various settings. Being cognizant of these risks is the first step toward prevention. Reports indicate that violence against transgender people is widespread, underscoring the importance of vigilance.

Human Rights Watch

- **Safety Planning**: Develop strategies to enhance safety, such as avoiding areas known for discriminatory incidents and establishing check-in routines when apart.

- **Legal Protections**: Familiarize yourselves with local laws regarding discrimination and hate crimes. Advocate for policies that protect transgender individuals and report any incidents to authorities.

- **Support Networks**: Engage with community organizations that offer resources and support for trans individuals. These networks can provide assistance and a sense of community.

- **Advocacy**: Actively challenge anti-transgender remarks and support transgender rights. Visible support can foster acceptance and deter discriminatory behavior.

<u>Transgender Equality</u>

By proactively addressing family dynamics and being vigilant about safety considerations, you can create a supportive environment that nurtures your relationship and promotes the well-being of your trans partner.

7 JOY AND SUCCESS

Celebrating trans joy and success is essential in fostering understanding, dismantling stereotypes, and promoting inclusivity. By highlighting positive representations and building inclusive communities, we can inspire and uplift both trans individuals and society as a whole.

Positive Representation: Showcasing Success Stories

Trans individuals have made significant contributions across various fields, serving as beacons of resilience and achievement. Sharing their stories not only challenges misconceptions but also provides role models for others.

- **Arts and Entertainment**: Trans artists have continually shaped the cultural landscape. For instance, the compilation album TRANSA highlights the contributions of trans, nonbinary, and queer artists, emphasizing their influence in music.

<u>Them</u>

- **Personal Narratives**: Individual stories of trans joy in relationships offer profound insights. Research has shown that trans women find joy in relationships through mutual support and understanding, challenging one-dimensional depictions of their experiences.

<u>Greater Good Science Center</u>

- **Advocacy and Activism**: Figures like Cecilia Gentili have left enduring legacies in activism, art, and community building, exemplifying the power of trans leadership in social justice movements.

<u>Them</u>

Highlighting these narratives fosters a more nuanced understanding of trans experiences, moving beyond adversity to celebrate achievements and joy.

Building Inclusive Communities: Strategies and Initiatives

Creating supportive networks that celebrate trans identities and relationships is vital for societal progress. Inclusive communities provide safe spaces for expression, connection, and growth.

- **Support Groups and Networks**: Establishing groups where trans individuals and allies can share experiences and resources fosters solidarity. These networks offer emotional support and practical assistance, reinforcing a sense of belonging.

- **Inclusive Policies and Practices**: Organizations can implement trans-inclusive nondiscrimination policies, ensuring equitable treatment. Crafting such policies and promoting them within the organization cultivates an inclusive culture.

<u>Transgender Equality</u>

- **Community Events and Celebrations**: Hosting events like Transgender Day of Visibility uplifts trans contributions and fosters community engagement. Such events provide platforms for trans voices and promote awareness.

<u>BBC Radio</u>

- **Educational Programs**: Developing curricula that include trans histories and contributions educates the broader community, promoting empathy and understanding.

By actively participating in or creating these initiatives, individuals and organizations contribute to a more inclusive society that honors and celebrates trans identities.

The Impact of Positive Representation and Inclusive Communities

Emphasizing trans joy and success has profound effects:

- **Empowerment**: Positive representation empowers trans individuals to embrace their identities and pursue their aspirations.

- **Education**: Sharing success stories educates the public, reducing ignorance and fostering acceptance.

- **Policy Influence**: Visible achievements can influence policymakers to enact laws that protect and support trans rights.

- **Community Building**: Inclusive communities provide essential support networks, enhancing the well-being of trans individuals.

Celebrating trans joy and success is not merely an act of recognition but a catalyst for broader societal change. By uplifting these narratives and fostering inclusive environments, we pave the way for a more equitable and compassionate world.

8 NAVIGATING RELATIONSHIPS

Navigating relationships with trans women requires access to comprehensive resources and literature that foster understanding and support. This chapter provides a curated list of organizations and recommended readings to assist individuals and their partners in building informed and empathetic connections.

Support Organizations

Engaging with organizations dedicated to the well-being of trans individuals and their partners can offer invaluable support. These organizations provide resources ranging from counseling services to educational materials:

- **LGBT Foundation**: Offers a variety of resources for trans and non-binary individuals, including support groups and healthcare guidance. Their trans resources are designed to help individuals achieve hope and joy.

<u>LGBT Foundation</u>

- **OurPath**: Focuses on providing information and support for partners of trans people, addressing the unique experiences and challenges they may face. Their resources aim to help partners move through shock, grief, and trauma toward a fulfilling new life.

<u>Our Path</u>

- **FFLAG (Families and Friends of Lesbians and Gays)**: A UK-based organization offering support to families and friends of LGBTQ+ individuals, including trans people. They provide resources to help families understand and support their trans loved ones.

<u>FFLAG</u>

- **Mermaids**: Supports transgender, non-binary, and gender-diverse children and young people, as well as their families. They offer helpline services, web chat support, and resources to assist families in navigating gender identity issues.

<u>Mermaids UK</u>

- **MindOut**: A mental health service run by and for LGBTQ+ people, providing support for trans and gender-diverse individuals. They offer online support, advocacy, and peer mentoring to promote mental well-being.

<u>MindOut</u>

These organizations serve as pillars of support, offering safe spaces and resources to navigate the complexities of relationships involving trans individuals.

Recommended Literature

Delving into literature that explores trans experiences and relationships can deepen understanding and empathy. The following books and articles are recommended:

- **"Whipping Girl: A Transsexual Woman on Sexism and the Scapegoating of Femininity" by Julia Serano**: A groundbreaking work that examines the intersection of transphobia and sexism, offering insights into the experiences of trans women.

<u>LGBTQ Nation</u>

- **"She's Not There: A Life in Two Genders" by Jennifer Finney Boylan**: One of the first works to present the transgender experience from a literary perspective, exploring themes of love, sex, gender, and identity.

<u>Penguin Random House</u>

- **"Detransition, Baby" by Torrey Peters**: A bold novel that explores the complexities of gender, relationships, and parenthood, offering a nuanced portrayal of trans experiences.

<u>Books and Bao</u>

- **"Gender Euphoria" edited by Laura Kate Dale**: An anthology that shifts focus from gender dysphoria to the joy found in gender affirmation, featuring essays from various writers.

<u>Book Riot</u>

- **"Transgender Warriors: Making History from Joan of Arc to Dennis Rodman" by Leslie Feinberg**: A historical exploration of gender non-conformity, highlighting trans figures throughout history.

<u>Queer In The World</u>

- **"Beyond the Gender Binary" by Alok Vaid-Menon**: An accessible introduction to understanding non-binary identities, challenging societal norms around gender.

<u>Queer In The World</u>

- **"Transgender Reading List for Adults" by PFLAG**: A curated list of books and articles that provide diverse perspectives on transgender experiences, suitable for those seeking a deeper understanding.

<u>PFLAG</u>

Engaging with these readings can foster a more profound comprehension of trans identities and the dynamics of relationships involving trans individuals.

Additional Resources

Beyond organizations and literature, consider the following avenues to enhance understanding and support:

- **Online Communities and Forums**: Participating in online discussions can provide real-time insights and shared experiences. Platforms like Reddit have communities such as r/transgender and r/asktransgender where individuals share stories and advice.

- **Workshops and Seminars**: Attending events focused on trans issues and relationships can offer interactive learning experiences. Organizations like the Human Rights Campaign often host educational events and webinars.

- **Counseling and Support Groups**: Engaging in therapy or support groups can provide personalized guidance. Many mental health professionals specialize in gender identity issues and can offer tailored support.

- **Advocacy and Allyship Training**: Participating in allyship programs can equip individuals with the tools to support trans partners effectively. Programs like those offered by GLAAD provide resources on being an effective ally.

By utilizing these resources, individuals can cultivate informed, empathetic, and supportive relationships with trans women, contributing to a more inclusive and understanding society.

9 COMPREHENSIVE APPROACH

Understanding and nurturing relationships with trans women necessitates a comprehensive approach that encompasses both emotional and practical dimensions. By integrating personal anecdotes, case studies, and expert insights, we can gain diverse perspectives and practical advice to foster relationships grounded in understanding, respect, and love that transcend societal barriers.

Personal Anecdotes: Navigating Love and Identity

Personal stories offer invaluable insights into the lived experiences of trans women and their partners, highlighting the challenges and triumphs they encounter.

- **Bee and Joe's Journey**: Bee, a trans woman, and Joe, a cisgender man, share a loving relationship that defies societal expectations. Their story underscores the importance of open communication and mutual respect. Joe's unwavering support during Bee's transition exemplifies the strength of their bond, illustrating that love can flourish when partners embrace each other's authentic selves.

BBC

- **Tadhg's Transformation**: Tadhg McMullan, a trans man, recounts his journey of coming out at 39 and the impact on his relationships. His narrative highlights the significance of self-acceptance and the role of supportive partners in navigating the complexities of gender identity.

BBC

These personal accounts demonstrate that, despite societal challenges, relationships involving trans individuals can thrive through understanding, communication, and support.

Case Studies: Insights into Trans Relationships
Academic case studies provide structured analyses of relationships involving trans individuals, offering deeper understanding of their dynamics.

- **Couple Dynamics During Transition**: A study examining couples where one partner transitions reveals that many relationships endure and even strengthen post-transition. Key factors contributing to this resilience include open communication, counseling, and a shared commitment to the relationship. The study emphasizes that transitions can be navigated successfully when both partners are dedicated to understanding and supporting each other.

Quod

- **Social Work and Trans Individuals**: Research into social work practices with trans individuals highlights the importance of inclusive assessment tools and representation. By incorporating trans-specific considerations into social work, practitioners can better support trans individuals and their relationships, ensuring that services are tailored to their unique needs.

Community Care

These case studies underscore the importance of tailored support and the positive impact of informed, empathetic approaches in fostering healthy relationships involving trans individuals.

Expert Insights: Building Respectful and Supportive Relationships

Experts in the field offer guidance on fostering relationships with trans women that are respectful, supportive, and enriching.

- **Effective Communication**: Using correct pronouns and names is fundamental. Misgendering can cause significant distress and erode trust. Experts advise asking for and consistently using a person's chosen pronouns to validate their identity and demonstrate respect.

Everyday Feminism

- **Navigating Conversations About Gender Identity**: Engaging in discussions about gender identity requires sensitivity. Educating oneself about transgender experiences reduces the burden on trans individuals to explain their identity. Respecting privacy and allowing individuals to share what they're comfortable with is crucial.

<u>Everyday Feminism</u>

- **Active Listening and Empathy**: Being present in conversations, reflecting on what's shared, and showing empathy are vital. These practices foster understanding and connection, allowing partners to support each other effectively.

<u>Everyday Feminism</u>

- **Establishing Trust**: Trust is built by respecting boundaries, ensuring confidentiality, and being consistent and reliable. Supporting a partner's autonomy in decisions about their life and identity further strengthens trust.

<u>Everyday Feminism</u>

By integrating these expert recommendations, individuals can cultivate relationships with trans women that are affirming and resilient.

Addressing Societal Barriers

Societal barriers, such as discrimination and prejudice, pose significant challenges to relationships involving trans women. Understanding and addressing these barriers is essential.

- **Discrimination and Prejudice**: Trans women often face societal biases, including transmisogyny and intersectional discrimination. These biases can strain relationships and impact mental health. Recognizing and actively combating these prejudices is crucial for fostering supportive relationships.

Everyday Feminism

- **Advocacy and Allyship**: Being an ally involves more than passive support; it requires proactive engagement and advocacy. Educating oneself, using affirming language, providing emotional support, and advocating for trans rights are key components of effective allyship.

Everyday Feminism

By addressing societal barriers and committing to allyship, individuals can create environments where relationships with trans women can thrive.

Conclusion

Building meaningful relationships with trans women involves a multifaceted approach that addresses both emotional and practical aspects. Personal anecdotes and case studies provide real-world insights, while expert guidance offers practical advice for navigating these relationships. By fostering understanding, respect, and love, and by actively challenging societal barriers, we can cultivate relationships that transcend societal norms and celebrate authentic connections.

10 MEANINGFUL RELATIONSHIPS

Building meaningful relationships with trans women requires a comprehensive understanding of both emotional and practical aspects. Incorporating personal anecdotes, case studies, and expert insights can provide diverse perspectives and practical advice, fostering understanding, respect, and love that transcends societal barriers.

Personal Anecdotes: Navigating Love and Identity

Personal stories offer invaluable insights into the lived experiences of trans women and their partners, highlighting the challenges and triumphs they encounter.

- **Marian and Michael's Journey:** Marian, a trans woman from Tondo Manila, Philippines, and Michael, a cisgender man from Malaga, Washington, USA, met online in September 2017. After several visits over a year, they solidified their relationship, demonstrating that love can flourish across distances and societal expectations. Their openness about their relationship serves as an example of the rewarding nature of partnerships with trans women.

My Transgender Date

- **Ellaine and David's Story:** Ellaine, a trans woman from the Philippines, initiated contact with David through a dating website. After six months of communication, David traveled to the Philippines and proposed to Ellaine. Their story underscores the importance of initiative and communication in building relationships.

These narratives illustrate that, despite societal challenges, relationships involving trans women can thrive through understanding, communication, and support.

Case Studies: Insights into Trans Relationships

Academic case studies provide structured analyses of relationships involving trans individuals, offering deeper understanding of their dynamics.

- **Overcoming Obstacles:** Success Stories from Trans Couples: This study highlights inspiring success stories from trans couples who have navigated societal barriers, legislative hurdles, and personal battles. Their journeys reflect the power of love and resilience, emphasizing that with mutual support, trans relationships can emerge stronger.

<u>**Transamorous**</u>

- **Trans Women and Cisgender Dating:** Struggles and Benefits: This research delves into the unique challenges trans women face when dating cisgender partners, often stemming from societal expectations and stereotypes. By recognizing these challenges, both partners can work together to build a strong, supportive foundation for their relationship.

<u>**My Transgender Cupid**</u>

These case studies underscore the importance of tailored support and the positive impact of informed, empathetic approaches in fostering healthy relationships involving trans individuals.

Expert Insights: Building Respectful and Supportive Relationships

Experts in the field offer guidance on fostering relationships with trans women that are respectful, supportive, and enriching.

- **Effective Communication:** Using correct pronouns and names is fundamental. Misgendering can cause significant distress and erode trust. Experts advise asking for and consistently using a person's chosen pronouns to validate their identity and demonstrate respect.

Toby Barron Therapy

- **Navigating Conversations About Gender Identity:** Engaging in discussions about gender identity requires sensitivity. Educating oneself about transgender experiences reduces the burden on trans individuals to explain their identity. Respecting privacy and allowing individuals to share what they're comfortable with is crucial.

Toby Barron Therapy

- **Active Listening and Empathy:** Being present in conversations, reflecting on what's shared, and showing empathy are vital. These practices foster understanding and connection, allowing partners to support each other effectively.

<u>**Toby Barron Therapy**</u>

- **Establishing Trust:** Trust is built by respecting boundaries, ensuring confidentiality, and being consistent and reliable. Supporting a partner's autonomy in decisions about their life and identity further strengthens trust.

<u>**Toby Barron Therapy**</u>

By integrating these expert recommendations, individuals can cultivate relationships with trans women that are affirming and resilient.

Addressing Societal Barriers

Societal barriers, such as discrimination and prejudice, pose significant challenges to relationships involving trans women. Understanding and addressing these barriers is essential.

- **Discrimination and Prejudice:** Trans women often face societal biases, including transmisogyny and intersectional discrimination. These biases can strain relationships and impact mental health. Recognizing and actively combating these prejudices is crucial for fostering supportive relationships.

Toby Barron Therapy

- **Advocacy and Allyship:** Being an ally involves more than passive support; it requires proactive engagement and advocacy. Educating oneself, using affirming language, providing emotional support, and advocating for trans rights are key components of effective allyship.

Toby Barron Therapy

By addressing societal barriers and committing to allyship, individuals can create environments where relationships with trans women can thrive.

Conclusion

Building meaningful relationships with trans women involves a multifaceted approach that addresses both emotional and practical aspects. Personal anecdotes and case studies provide real-world insights, while expert guidance offers practical advice for navigating these relationships. By fostering understanding, respect, and love, and by actively challenging societal barriers, we can cultivate relationships that transcend societal norms and celebrate authen

Embracing Authenticity: Building Meaningful
Relationships with Trans Women

ISBN: 9798301927508
Cover design by Lynnie Ceniza
Interior design and formatting by Lynnie Ceniza
Published by Arthur Crandon Publishing
Visit our website: Arthurcrandon.co.uk
DISCLAIMER
The information provided in this book is for general
informational purposes only. It does not constitute legal,
financial, or professional advice. While every effort has
been made to ensure accuracy, the author and publisher
assume no responsibility for errors or omissions. Readers
should consult with appropriate professionals for specific
advice tailored to their individual circumstances.
First Edition: August 2024

If you enjoyed this book, please consider leaving a review – your feedback may help others to discover the book.

If you send me a screenshot of your review, I will send you a copy of another of my Self-Help books.

You can email me on
ac@arthurcrandon.co.uk

To leave a review – just go back to the book on Amazon and scroll down – the link to leave a review is on the left hand side.

Thanks, and very best wishes.